Between Good and Evil

By

D. M. Larson

doug@freedrama.net

MONOLOGUE FROM ANOTHER WORLD

(A single light appears. An alien, who looks very much like you and me, appears. The alien can speak to the audience or use props that represent different types of people in the universe, arranging them to as an example of what is being talked about)

ALIEN

I am not of your world but I know everything about you. Because everywhere I go in the universe, everyone is the same. Everyone is dreaming and wishing on stars. Everyone is seeking a better life for themselves or for others. And that's how the universe is divided. Those who want for themselves... and those who want for others. What do you want? What type of life form are you? Are you here to get hold of the most wonderful thing you can imagine and hang on to it as long as possible? Or do you want to leave the universe a little better off than it was before you were in existence? We all chose whether we know it or not. We all decide to give or take. And sooner or later we all learn what is at the center of the universe. Is it you or is it me? Or is there some other incredible secret waiting for us at the core of it all?

(Lights come up on an alien planet)

ALIEN (CONT.)

Do we explore for knowledge? Or explore for gain? Are we seeking to make the universe better or do our actions cause others pain? Some will choose pain while others fight for what's right. While some will gain a special new insight.

TOUCHED BY AN ALIEN

A couple of space explorers, Captain and Commander, are
sitting relaxed among the rocks looking at their electronic
devices taking and recording readings. A couple of other
space explorers, Cadet and Grunt, run past behind them
yelling/screaming being chased by strange aliens. Captain
and Commander look at each other and shrug. Aliens run back
across with Grunt and Cadet chasing them.

                    CAPTAIN
          Care for some tea, Commander?

                    COMMANDER
          Why yes, Captain. That would be
          lovely.

Captain pours Commander some tea. Alien runs by and knocks
it from the Captain's hand and leaves. Cadet and Grunt
chase alien.

                    CAPTAIN
          How rude.

                    COMMANDER
          I vote for sub-intelligent life
          forms.

                    CAPTAIN
          Noted. They do appear to be quite
          savage.

Grunt and Cadet bring in one of the aliens they've captured.

                    CADET
          Yee-haw! We got one!

                    GRUNT
          On your knees, maggot!

Grunt forces alien on to its knees in front of the Commander
and Captain. Commander waves a device in front of it.

                    COMMANDER
          Scanning... imaging... OH!

                    CAPTAIN
          What is it?

                    COMMANDER
          Special alert from the
          Inter-galactic shopping
          network. That new phase scanner is
          50% off this week.

                                        (CONTINUED)

Explorers gather around Commander. Alien sneaks off during following.

                    CAPTAIN
          Buy it! Buy it!

                    COMMANDER
          I love this new app. Makes
          purchasing so much easier. The
          deals I'm finding are amazing.

                    CAPTAIN
          Uh... which one of you was watching
          the alien?

Cadet and Grunt look at each other. Grunt punches Cadet.

                    CADET
          Ow!

                    GRUNT
          Get moving!

                    CADET
          I'm an officer. You're supposed to
          listen to me.

                    GRUNT
          You're like 12. How did you get in
          officer training?

                    CADET
          I was on this colony ship and
          impressed one of the Space
          Explorers with my incredible
          intelligence.

                    CAPTAIN
          And it doesn't hurt that your
          father is an Admiral.

Commander laughs.

                    GRUNT
          Move it!

                    CADET
          I'm so reporting you.

Cadet and Grunt run after alien.

(CONTINUED)

                         COMMANDER
          Commander's vlog... Spacedate
          Niner-Ought-Ocho-Alpha...

                         CAPTAIN
          You so have something in your
          teeth.

                         COMMANDER
          Thanks.

Commander uses video screen to check teeth.

                         CAPTAIN
          I think you're still
          recording. Streaming live.

                         COMMANDER
          Great.

                         CAPTAIN
          Think we can get those aliens to
          sign the Galaxy Confederation
          Charter?

                         COMMANDER
          I have ways of making that happen.

                         CAPTAIN
          Promise me you won't chop off one
          of their hands again. That was so
          gross.

                         COMMANDER
          Worked didn't it? Hand print
          signature was a sure thing after
          that.

                         CAPTAIN
          But you got alien goo all over the
          WeePad. It still doesn't work
          right.

                         COMMANDER
          Fine. Do it the hard way.

Cadet and Grunt drag in an alien (can be the same or
different one).

                         CAPTAIN
          Hello, good alien. Please sit.

Grunt forces alien down.

                                              (CONTINUED)

> CAPTAIN (CONT.)
> Care for some tea?

> COMMANDER
> This is going to take forever.

> GRUNT
> Want me to do the hand thing?

Grunt pulls out a huge knife and holds up alien's hand.

> COMMANDER
> The captain here doesn't like that.

> CADET
> That's against our Galactic
> Confederation Code!

Grunt laughs and puts knife away.

> GRUNT
> We're a long way from the GCC,
> Cadet.

Cadet points proudly to a badge on uniform.

> CADET
> Where-ever you see this badge, the
> GCC is the law and I shall...

Grunt grabs the badge off Cadet's uniform and tosses it away
as far as possible.

> CADET (CONT.)
> Hey!

Cadet goes after it.

> CAPTAIN
> So, my friend. What kind of tea do
> you like? I can generate any
> number of flavors.

> GRUNT
> Make it extra hot.

> CAPTAIN
> No torture.

> GRUNT
> Commander?

(CONTINUED)

                    COMMANDER
          Listen to the Captain.

                    GRUNT
          I'm so transferring after this
          mission.

                    CAPTAIN
          So savage. I know none of this
          means anything to you but I simply
          need your hand print. It says you
          agree to the GCC and your planet
          and all the resources here will
          belong to us. In return, we will
          give you this shiny new GCC
          badge! Each one is uniquely
          engraved with an unduplicated
          number and a holographic image of
          our supreme leader.

Captain holds out badge to alien.

                    CAPTAIN (CONT.)
          It's shiny.

Alien slowly takes and looks at it.

                    CAPTAIN (CONT.)
          Pretty.

Alien throws it at Captain.

                    CAPTAIN (CONT.)
          My eye! It hit me in the eye!

Grunt is laughing. Commander grabs the alien's hand and
sticks its hand print on to the WeePad.

                    COMMANDER
          Done. Let it go.

                    GRUNT
          No souvenirs?

                    COMMANDER
          Gross. No.

Grunt let's go of alien but it doesn't run. Alien goes up
to Captain who is still crumpled over. It touches the
Captain's wound. Captain flinches. The alien spits on its
own hand and then touches the hand to the Captain's eye.

>   CAPTAIN
>   Hey! Oh... that feels good.

Alien pulls away and Captain's eye is okay. Captain looks
in amazement.

>   CAPTAIN (CONT.)
>   Thank you.

Alien walks away.

>   COMMANDER
>   That was different.

>   CAPTAIN
>   Quite.

>   COMMANDER
>   I think your eye is a slightly
>   different color now.

>   CAPTAIN
>   I can see better too.

>   COMMANDER
>   This requires further study.

>   CAPTAIN
>   We'll report to the GCC and get
>   authorized for a return voyage.

>   COMMANDER
>   To the shuttle?

>   CAPTAIN
>   To the shuttle.

>   GRUNT
>   Totally asking for a transfer. I
>   didn't get to kill anything.

They exit and a rocket blast is heard. After a few moments
Cadet returns.

>   CADET
>   Where did everybody go?

Cadet wanders around and sits sadly and wraps his arms
around himself. ALIEN narrator returns.

>   ALIEN
>   All of us are born innocent babies,
>   ready to be shaped. But others are
>   (MORE)

                                              (CONTINUED)

                         ALIEN (cont'd)
          reborn as a reaction to what we
          experience in life. Some of us
          grow stronger while other shrink in
          fear. And in this lowest moment,
          this is when we forge a new path in
          our future.

Cadet jumps up and throws a rock at where the space
explorers left from.

                         CADET
          I hate you... I hate you all!

                         ALIEN
          For some a miracle happens.

Cadet picks up another rock and it glows in his hand.

                         CADET
          What is this?

                         ALIEN
          A small discovery has a big impact.

All the aliens start gathering around CADET. He holds up
the glowing rock and they cower. They start making humming
noises and bow before him. CADET starts to smile.

                         CADET
          Yes... yes... bow before me. Bow
          before my might and glory. Worship
          me!

The aliens all motion for him to follow and he does.

                         ALIEN
          There are important moments in our
          lives where we must make a
          choice. A choice to be good or a
          choice to be evil. If others
          follow, where will you lead
          them? To a better life or to a
          life that's only better for
          you? That's how heroes are
          made. They are the ones who devote
          themselves to others, wanting to
          change what is wrong and make
          things right.

                    END OF SCENE

PROTECTO (KID HERO)

                    PROTECTO
          I've always dreamed of being a
          hero. I've tried everything to
          become super. I let a spider bite
          me... no spider powers; just lots
          of itching. I tried standing too
          close to the microwave oven hoping
          the radiation would change
          me. Nothing. And I got in trouble
          for making so many bags of
          popcorn. But I took it all to
          school and had a popcorn party. I
          was a hero that day. So I guess it
          kinda worked.

          I love being a hero. I love
          helping people. I love making them
          happy. And I hate bad guys. I
          hate creeps who hurt people.

          There's this kid at school... he is
          always hurting everyone. I am sick
          of him hurting us. I just need
          those super powers. I need
          something that will make him stop.

Lost in thought.

                    PROTECTO (CONT.)
          Maybe if I eat more of the school
          lunches. They look
          radioactive. If I get enough green
          hotdogs and brown ketchup in me...
          something is bound to happen.

Nods in approval.

                    PROTECTO (CONT.)
          And I need a catch phrase like
          "gonna smoosh me a baddie"... and a
          cool costume... actually last time
          I was in the bathroom, I saw the
          perfect superhero
          name. Protecto! Instead of a
          telephone booth like superman, I
          could use a bathroom stall and
          those Protecto seat covers could be
          a cape... and make a toilet paper
          mask. Nothing scares bad guys more
          than bathroom stuff.

Thinks then frowns.

(CONTINUED)

                         PROTECTO (CONT.)
                    Or maybe it will really make them
                    want to give me a swirly. I better
                    rethink this.

                         END OF SCENE

STUNG

                         ALIEN
                    Being a hero isn't easy. We might
                    want to help others but sometimes
                    we are too weak and feel helpless
                    at times. But the spirit must
                    remain strong if we are to achieve
                    a greater good.

June is wandering around looking at flowers.

                         ALIEN (CONT.)
                    In life, even small acts of
                    kindness can create a hero. There
                    doesn't need to be a meteor falling
                    toward your planet for a hero to
                    emerge.

June dances around happily and decides to take her shoes off
and dance some more.

                         ALIEN (CONT.)
                    Even the smallest crisis can give
                    us a chance to be a hero in the
                    lives of others.

Alien exits.

June screams! She falls on the ground holding her
foot. She shakes her leg and screams some more.

                         JUNE
                    AH!

Protecto runs out to see what's wrong.

                         PROTECTO
                    What happened?

                         JUNE
                    I got stung by a bee... on the
                    foot...

                                                        (CONTINUED)

                    PROTECTO
          Let me see.

June flops down and holds up her foot.

                    PROTECTO (CONT.)
          Okay, let me get the stinger
          out. I hear if you can get it out
          without squeezing the little venom
          bag then it won't hurt as much.

                    JUNE
          Ow! Ow! Ow! Get it out!

June is shaking her foot.

                    PROTECTO
          Hold still!

June tries to stop struggling. Protecto carefully gets it
with one finger.

                    PROTECTO (CONT.)
          There.

                    JUNE
          Still hurts.

She shakes her foot at him. Protecto struggles and then
holds her leg still again and looks.

                    PROTECTO
          Looks like there is a bit of
          stinger in there still.

                    JUNE
          Get it out!

                    PROTECTO
          I'm going to need to tweezers or
          something.

                    JUNE
          Get some tweezers!

                    PROTECTO
          Okay, okay!

Protecto runs off. *Various people can walk by and try to
ignore June and make gestures and faces if desired* Molly
walks by and sees June on her back moaning and holding her
foot in the air.

                                              (CONTINUED)

                    MOLLY
          Uh... you okay?

                    JUNE
          No...

                    MOLLY
          Can I help?

                    JUNE
          I don't know...

                    MOLLY
          Tell me what's wrong and I'll see
          what I can do?

                    JUNE
          I got stung by a bee.

                    MOLLY
          How did you get stung?

                    JUNE
          I stopped to smell the roses.

                    MOLLY
          What?

                    JUNE
          You know how they tell you to stop
          and smell the roses?

                    MOLLY
          They?

                    JUNE
          Well, sometimes you hear that.

                    MOLLY
          You do?

                    JUNE
          Oh geez, never mind.

                    MOLLY
          Do bee stings make people cranky?

                    JUNE
          Yes!

                    MOLLY
          Oh... so why were you barefoot?

                         JUNE
            Because I wanted to be one with
            nature! I love nature!

June starts ripping at the grass and flowers and throws them
in the air.

                         JUNE (CONT.)
            Weeee! Weee! Weee! OW!

June has hurt her hand now.

                         MOLLY
            What happened?

                         JUNE
            Nature gave me some more good
            loving! Thorn.

June sucks on her thumb.

                         MOLLY
            Nature doesn't love you back.

                         JUNE
            What did I ever do to nature? I
            try to be good. I try to leave a
            small carbon footprint. I have a
            hybrid car. I use recycled toilet
            paper...

                         MOLLY
            Recycled toilet paper... sorry, but
            that just sounds gross.

                         JUNE
            It is just recycled paper... it
            wasn't used in a toilet before...
            well, I don't think so...

                         MOLLY
            Now I don't feel so good.

                         JUNE
            Don't like potty talk?

                         MOLLY
            Not really. Poop scares me.

                         JUNE
            That's too bad because I think you
            stepped in some.

(CONTINUED)

                    MOLLY
          Uh! Nature strikes again... see
          ya...

Molly exits and drags her foot/shoe on the ground trying to
get some poop off. June sighs... a little old man, Don,
shuffles out. June ignores him. Don pokes her with his
walking stick/cane.

                    JUNE
          Hey!

                    DON
          "Hey you!" back. Get off my lawn.

                    JUNE
          This your lawn?

                    DON
          Yup... get off.

                    JUNE
          But I can't walk... I'm injured...

She holds her foot up to Don. He gets out his glasses and
looks at her foot closely. He smells something bad and
backs away.

                    DON
          Wow, that's quite a stink.

                    JUNE
          That's not my foot... some dog
          pooped on your lawn.

                    DON
          Dag-nabbit! Darn frickin' dogs!

                    JUNE
          Such language in front of a lady.

                    DON
          You're just a hippy. Did you rip
          up my flowers?

                    JUNE
          Um...

                    DON
          You hippies ain't got no respect
          for property!

(CONTINUED)

                    JUNE
          Look... don't get all worked up
          now...

Don grabs his chest and falls on top of June.

                    JUNE (CONT.)
          He got worked up.

Protecto runs back in with tweezers.

                    PROTECTO
          I got the...

Protecto sees old man Don on top of June.

                    PROTECTO (CONT.)
          Um... I'm not sure the tweezers can
          remove that...

                    JUNE
          Get him off!

Protecto picks up Don and struggles with him and ends up
falling and having Don on top of him. June looks and holds
up her foot.

                    JUNE (CONT.)
          Can you get the thorn out now...
          please?

Molly crosses the stage dragging her foot.

                    MOLLY
          Pooh! Hate the smell of pooh!

Lights fade to black.

                    END OF SCENE

Alien enters as Protecto helps June off the stage.

                    ALIEN
          Kindness is one of the greatest
          super powers. A kind heart can
          make the world a better place for
          those around us.

16.

BLINDED BY THE KNIGHT

It is evening at a comic book store. If an instant backdrop
is possible, there can be several posters and novelties
decorating this. On wheels, a large cabinet with signs
stating types of comics. The comics are facing away from the
audience. A Ninja pokes up from behind the cabinet and
looks around. She sneaks around the book shelf and hides
behind it (the audience can see her still). Joe walks
upstage of the book case. She grabs a comic over the shelf
with snakelike speed. Joe stops and looks around but
doesn't see anything and shrugs. She sneaks away right
behind him but he doesn't notice her.

Alien speaks as Howard enters reading a comic book.

                    ALIEN
          There's this young man named
          Howard... he's a good kid... but
          he's shy and can't talk to girls.

Ashley walks by Howard who gets all nervous and hides his
face behind the comic book.

                    ALIEN (CONT.)
          And there's a princess... well, she
          was always told she was a
          princess... and she got whatever
          she wanted. She loves pretty
          things...

Ninja appears with something shiny like jewelry and dangles
it by Ashley.

                    ASHLEY
          Ooh! Shiny!

Ashley whips out her credit card and grabs the jewel. Ninja
takes the card and goes. Howard peeks over the comic at
Ashley.

                    ALIEN
          These two need to learn a lesson
          and a mysterious person, a hero of
          sorts, plans to give them a whole
          new outlook on life.

Alien exits. Joe goes over to Ashley.

                    JOE
          You like kryptonite jewelry huh?

(CONTINUED)

                        ASHLEY
          As long as it is big and flashy, I
          like it lots. Where's the little
          princess's room?

                        JOE
          Back down the hall. Look for the
          Supergirl poster.

                        ASHLEY
          How come it is super-<u>girl</u> and then
          super-<u>man</u>? Isn't that sexist?

                        JOE
          Uh... sure.

                        ASHLEY
          Well, stop doing that.

                        JOE
          Yeah... I'll call my friends at DC
          comics right now and get them to
          change that.

                        ASHLEY
          Good. See, that's why I won the
          title Miss Politically Correct last
          year.

                        JOE
          How many people were in that
          contest?

                        ASHLEY
          Doesn't matter. The important
          thing is that the right person won.

Ashley exits. Howard rushes over to Joe and lowers his
comic.

                        HOWARD
          Is that who I think it is?

                        JOE
          Yup, that's Ashley Anderson, beauty
          queen. Miss Teen Walla Walla, Miss
          Pet Lover, Miss Apple Pie... She's
          been the Miss of everything I
          think.

                        HOWARD
          What is she doing here?

(CONTINUED)

                    JOE
She's here to do a photo shoot.
She's endorsing the store and then
we're endorsing her. See, they
think she is a sure thing to win
Miss Washington this year and if
she can win Miss America, then this
sponsorship will be gold. My
online sales will skyrocket. And
she gets someone to pay some of the
bills.

                    HOWARD
But how?

                    JOE
She's my cousin.

                    HOWARD
You never told me that!

                    JOE
It's a family secret. I'm rather
embarrassed by her, but it might
finally be useful to know her.

                    HOWARD
I've always wanted to talk to her.

                    JOE
You want to talk to any woman.

Ashley comes out and Howard lifts his comic and goes to
hide. Joe goes to the front door and locks it.

                    JOE (CONT.)
I better lock the door before the
nerds start swarming.

                    ASHLEY
Ew... there's one now. He's
drooling on the window.

Joe hands her some money.

                    JOE
Here's your money. Be nice.

Ashley smiles and waves and blows a kiss.

                    JOE (CONT.)
I think you just killed that one.

                         ASHLEY
               Ready for the photo?

Joe is looking around for the camera.

                         JOE
               In a hurry? Big plans tonight?

                         ASHLEY
               My big plans are to be some where
               else.

Ninja puts camera near Joe unnoticed. Joe finds it.

                         JOE
               I want you wearing this sash and
               holding this comic book.

Joe gives sash to Ashley.

                         ASHLEY
               Miss All Knight?

                         JOE
               It's the name of the store "All
               Knight Novelty."

                         ASHLEY
               It sounds weird though.

                         JOE
               And here is the comic.

                         ASHLEY
               Ew! I don't wanna hold that. It's
               gross.

                         JOE
               But she's where the store gets the
               name from... Knight Princess...
               she's a warrior princess. I
               thought you liked princesses.

                         ASHLEY
               But look at her outfit. And what's
               she doing to that monster.

                         JOE
               I believe she is ripping that
               zombie a new one.

                    ASHLEY
          Ew!

                    JOE
          I'll look for one with a better
          cover.

Ninja sets out a comic and sprinkles something inside the
bag holding the comic. Joe finds it.

                    JOE (CONT.)
          Here we go. She is all dressed up
          for her coronation.

Joe sets up camera on tripod. Ashley looks at comic.

                    ASHLEY
          How can she fight in those
          clothes? Guy always have tons of
          armor but the warrior women wear
          practically nothing to protect
          their bodies.

                    JOE
          Good point. I'll shoot off another
          email to my friends at DC comics.

                    ASHLEY
          Ready?

                    JOE
          Take the comic out of the bag. The
          plastic is making a weird
          reflection. I'll be right back
          with another prop. We need
          something else to make the picture
          pop.

Joe exits. Ashley opens bag and ninja sneaks up and smashes
the end of it so the powder goes up in to Ashley's
face. She coughs violently as if she is going to die. Joe
runs back in and Howard cautiously approaches from his
hiding spot.

                    JOE
          What's going on?

                    HOWARD
          I don't know.

                    ASHLEY
          Something.. in the comic... my
          eyes!

                                                    (CONTINUED)

                        JOE
          What's wrong with your eyes?

                        ASHLEY
          I can't see... it got in my eyes...
          I need help.

                        JOE
          Wash it out with water.

                        HOWARD
          I'll get some.

Howard looks around.

                        ASHLEY
          It hurts so bad.

                        JOE
          Hang on... we'll wash it out.

Howard finds some bottled water.

                        HOWARD
          Here.

Joe splashes water on Ashley's face.

                        ASHLEY
          Hey! Idiot!

                        JOE
          That didn't help?

                        ASHLEY
          No! It still burns and I can't
          see.

                        JOE
          I'll call 911.

                        ASHLEY
          No, no, no. The press would be all
          over it. Get the family
          doctor. He'll come if you get
          daddy to call him.

                        JOE
          Fine. I'll call.

                        ASHLEY
          Don't leave me alone.

                    JOE
          Howard is here.

                    ASHLEY
          Howard?

                    JOE
          Howard Rogers. You know him from
          school.

                    ASHLEY
          No.

                    JOE
          Whatever... he's here... say "hi"
          Howard.

                    HOWARD
          Hi.

                    ASHLEY
          Thanks for being here to help,
          Howard.

Joe gets out his cell phone and goes upstage to call.

                    ASHLEY (CONT.)
          You're not that creepy guy outside
          that drooled on the window and
          fainted?

                    HOWARD
          No.

                    ASHLEY
          Oh, good. So how come I don't
          remember you from school?

                    HOWARD
          I... I don't know.

                    ASHLEY
          You're shy. That's why. I think
          that's so cute.

                    HOWARD
          Oh...

                    ASHLEY
          Take my hand please and lead me to
          a chair.

                                      (CONTINUED)

                    HOWARD
          Sure.

Howard looks very happy to be holding her hand. He walks
her to a chair (a spot with two chairs and a table).

                    JOE
          Your dad wants me to go pick up the
          doctor so he gets here quicker...
          you okay?

                    ASHLEY
          Howard will take good care of me.

Joe gives Howard a thumbs up. Howard smiles.

                    ASHLEY (CONT.)
          Thanks so much for helping me,
          Howard. I must look terrible.

                    HOWARD
          No, you look... good.

                    ASHLEY
          You're so sweet. Could you get my
          purse for me? I might have eye
          drops in there. That could help.

Ninja grabs her purse.

                    HOWARD
          Do you remember where you left it?

                    ASHLEY
          No.. silly me.. but I'm sure a
          smart guy like you can find it.

                    HOWARD
          Okay...

Howard searches around for purse as Ashley talks. During
the following, the ninja replaces eye drops with something
different that is the same shape but has scary symbol (skull
or Mr. Yuck sticker).

                    ASHLEY
          It's nice having a guy around who
          is so helpful. I could get used to
          having someone around who does
          things for me like this. I don't
          mean like a servant but as my
          special little helper. Especially
          if I'm blind now... you think I'll
                    (MORE)

                                              (CONTINUED)

                         ASHLEY (cont'd)
          be blind forever? I wonder if they
          have Miss Blind USA? Or maybe I'd
          be a shoe-in for Miss America if
          I'm blind. So this could be a
          blessing in disguise. You could be
          up there on stage with me guiding
          me around... I wonder if that's
          against the rules... I could get a
          cute little guide dog. People love
          animals too. A blind girl with a
          dog. I'd win for sure. Still
          haven't found my purse? I wonder
          where it went to.

Ninja has new eye drops in purse. She avoids Howard and
sneaks over to put it next to Ashley.

                         ASHLEY (CONT.)
          I hope Joe didn't take it. I have
          no clue why he would but you never
          know. You're such a good
          listener. I like that. Most the
          guys I hang out with just want to
          talk about themselves. They love
          talking about their bodies and
          their muscles and how they work out
          all the time or how they won the
          big game doing a touch basket or a
          win down or some such
          stupidity. Don't you hate it when
          someone always talks about
          themselves non-stop?

Ninja wants to kill Ashley by strangling her but Howard
turns to return and ninja hides. Howard sees the purse. He
goes up and gets it.

                         HOWARD
          I found it.

                         ASHLEY
          Great! I knew you could do
          it. Now find my eye drops.

Howard pulls weird silly things from her purse like bows,
ribbons, makeup, little stuffed animals until he finds
them.

                         HOWARD
          This kind of looks like eye drops
          but...

Ashley reaches out and Howard gives it to her.

                                                    (CONTINUED)

                          ASHLEY
                 That feels right.

                          HOWARD
                 You sure? It has...

                          ASHLEY
                 Of course I'm sure silly. Now
                 let's see if this helps my eyes.

Ninja watches. Ashley puts in the drops. Pause. Ashley
screams. Ninja does a victory dance as Ashley jumps up and
stumbles around in pain.

                          HOWARD
                 What happened?

                          ASHLEY
                 It burns! My eyes are on fire!

Ashley screams some more. Ninja hides being center
bookcase. Howard tries to grab her and calm her down but she
keeps punching him and knocking him down. They stumble in
to center bookcase where ninja is and it falls on her. Joe
and Doctor appear. NOTE: Doctor can be doubled with healing
Alien from "Touched by an Alien" or with Alien narrator.

                          JOE
                 What happened?!

                          HOWARD
                 She put... she wanted...

                          ASHLEY
                 The pain!

                          JOE
                 Your doctor is here, Ashley.

Ashley stops. She sniffles and cries a bit still.

                          ASHLEY
                 Oh... good... help me, Doc.

                          DOC
                 Sit down, please, Miss Anderson. I
                 have something to clean out your
                 eyes.

They help her sit. Doctor has some eye drops.

                                        (CONTINUED)

                    ASHLEY
          Will it hurt?

                    DOC
          Don't worry. Head back.

Doc puts in eye drops. After a few moments, she blinks.

                    ASHLEY
          I can see!

                    JOE
          Thankfully that's over.

                    DOC
          Home James.

                    JOE
          Joe.

                    DOC
          Whatever.

Joe to Howard.

                    JOE
          I bet he just made more in a minute
          than I make in a month. You and
          Ashley good?

                    HOWARD
          I think so.

                    JOE
          Cool. I'll take my time then.

Doc and Joe leave. Ashley gathers up her stuff from her
purse.

                    HOWARD
          Need any help?

                    ASHLEY
          You helped so much, Howard. Oh...

Ashley sees Howard and is disappointed.

                    HOWARD
          What's wrong?

                    ASHLEY
          Well, uh... you're not quite like I
          imagined.

                                              (CONTINUED)

                    HOWARD
          Oh... I see.

                    ASHLEY
          You were very nice and helpful. It
          was good to have your help.

                    HOWARD
          Okay.

                    ASHLEY
          I better go clean up. I bet I'm a
          mess.

Ashley goes back to bathroom. Howard is sad and sits.

                    HOWARD
          I can't believe it. I'm finally
          brave enough to talk to a girl but
          when she sees what I look like...

Ninja manages to pop her head out from under bookshelf.

                    NINJA
          Blind dates rarely work out.

Howard jumps up.

                    HOWARD
          Who said that?

                    NINJA
          Over here. Under the bookshelf.

                    HOWARD
          Are you okay?

                    NINJA
          I think so... I may have hurt my
          ankle.

                    HOWARD
          I'll get that off of you.

                    NINJA
          No hurry. I have plenty to read.

Howard manages to lift the bookshelf.

                    NINJA (CONT.)
          My knight in shining glasses. Come
          to rescue me. I hate being a
          damsel in distress.

                                        (CONTINUED)

He helps ninja over to the chairs.

                    HOWARD
          Let me see your leg.

                    NINJA
          Here.

She gives him her leg.

                    HOWARD
          Where does it hurt?

                    NINJA
          Oh, that's over here.

She gives him her other leg.

                    HOWARD
          We should wrap it in something.

                    NINJA
          You can use my mask.

Howard unwraps her mask. They pause a moment looking at
each other shyly.

                    HOWARD
          Mindy?

                    NINJA
          Hi.

                    HOWARD
          You're a ninja.

                    NINJA
          Ninja by night. Nerd by day.

Howard wraps her ankle.

                    HOWARD
          You're not that nerdy.

                    NINJA
          Not compared to you.

                    HOWARD
          Thanks.

                    NINJA
          I'm kidding.

                    HOWARD
          I know I'm a nerd.

                    NINJA
          But being a nerd is awesome.

                    HOWARD
          It is?

                    NINJA
          Yeah... all the rich and powerful
          people in the world are
          nerds. Bill Gates, Larry Ellison,
          Mark Zuckerberg. Nerds rule.

                    HOWARD
          And sports guy get all worn out and
          their bodies fall apart when they
          get old.

                    NINJA
          And the rich nerds marry
          supermodels.

                    HOWARD
          If they're like Ashley, then forget
          it.

                    NINJA
          They're all like Ashley.

                    HOWARD
          She thought I was fine until she
          saw what I looked like.

Ninja gets quiet.

                    NINJA
          I think you look good.

                    HOWARD
          What?

                    NINJA
          Nothing.

                    HOWARD
          You said something nice, didn't
          you?

                    NINJA
          Maybe.

They are quiet a moment.

(CONTINUED)

                    HOWARD
          So how come you're dressed as a
          ninja?

                    NINJA
          There are a few precious places in
          this world unspoiled by people like
          Ashley and this store is one of
          those places. I couldn't bare the
          thought of her ugly mug on a poster
          hanging in here next to these
          heroes. The heroes on these walls
          fight for justice and the greater
          good. To hang up some beauty
          pageant freak next to these symbols
          of greatest is an insult to all I
          believe in.

                    HOWARD
          Wow... well said.

                    NINJA
          I like talking to you, Howard.

                    HOWARD
          I like you too... I mean talking...
          I would like to talk.

Ninja laughs.

                    NINJA
          Take it easy, Howard.

                    HOWARD
          I'm an idiot.

                    NINJA
          You're cute actually.

                    HOWARD
          What? No...

                    NINJA
          Take me out for coffee or
          something.

                    HOWARD
          When?

                    NINJA
          Now.

                    HOWARD
          Okay.

                    NINJA
          Let me get my coat.

Ninja runs to back of store. Howard does a happy victory
dance. Ninja returns and he stops. She laughs.

                    NINJA (CONT.)
          Let's go.

As they go...

                    HOWARD
          Is it okay if I get tea? Coffee
          gives me the runs.

Ninja laughs.

                    NINJA
          Sure.

After a moment, there is a knocking in the back.

                    ASHLEY
          Hello? Anyone out
          there? Something is blocking the
          door and I can't get
          out. Anyone? Hello? Help!

Alien enters.

                    ALIEN
          Well, Howard didn't get the
          princess but he did end up with the
          future designer of the Waggit, a
          new gadget that everybody will want
          to buy. I'm not certain what it
          does but everyone will want it
          anyway. Sometimes love is what
          makes us do a little extra and be a
          hero in the life of another.

Alien is about to leave.

                    ASHLEY
          What about me?

                    ALIEN
          I nearly forgot. So did Ashley
          learn her lesson?

                         ASHLEY
              I hear voices. Who's out there?

                         ALIEN
              It's hard to say right now, but she
              has a long night ahead of her...
              maybe a light bulb moment will
              still happen to her. Until then,
              she'll simply... be in the dark.

Alien shuts off the lights by clapping his hands.

                         ASHLEY
              Oh, come on! You're kidding me
              right. Let me out of here!

                      END OF SCENE

Bookshelf is removed and replaces with a bench and large
Superman statue or Superman mural on backdrop.

                         ALIEN
              Love... a power that is difficult
              to control. Maybe of us seek, some
              of find it unsure how to harness
              this amazing power and other lose
              it, leading to emptiness. But we
              never stop searching for this
              special power that unites us even
              though it can also tear us
              apart. What would you do to find
              this power inside you? Would you
              give up everything and travel the
              world until you find it? How will
              your journey begin and end?

MAN OF METROPOLIS OR LOVE IN METROPOLIS

Lo is standing by a Superman statue and/or Superman mural
looking around at the surrounding town. Actors and even
dogs in Superman costumes can walk through the scene to
start the show if extras are available. She has a camera
and takes random pictures from weird angles. Kent has been
watching Lo. When she sits at a bench near the statue, she
appears sad and stressed. Kent moves in.

                         KENT
              Can I help you? You look a bit
              lost.

                    LO
          Is this Metropolis?

                    KENT
          The one and only.

                    LO
          I imagined something much bigger.

                    KENT
          Everyone does.

                    LO
          Looks more like Smallville.

                    KENT
          Superman fan?

                    LO
          Not really.

                    KENT
          That's a first. I bet you are the
          first person to visit this town who
          isn't a fan.

                    LO
          No other reason to come here?

                    KENT
          Nope.

                    LO
          So is Superman really from here?

                    KENT
          So they say... Never met him
          though.. Well maybe I have.. Met a
          lot of guys dressed like him... But
          none of them raced bullets or
          trains. And nobody flew here. We
          don't have an airport.

                    LO
          Huh? Oh... Joke.

(Does a courtesy laugh but it's not convincing)

                    KENT
          My name's Kent by the way.

(CONTINUED)

                    LO
          Kent? As in Clark Kent?

                    KENT
          If you are a male and born in this
          town, there is a good chance you'll
          be named Clark or Kent.

                    LO
          Oh dear... That has to be weird in
          school.

                    KENT
          Kal is gaining in popularity
          though.

                    LO
          Kal?

                    KENT
          For Kal-El... Superman's real name.

                    LO
          Is it required in this town to know
          all Superman facts or are you just
          a nerd?

                    KENT
          You can't help know this stuff
          here.. It's everywhere... Menu
          items, street names, constant puns
          in the newspaper...

                    LO
          Does it get annoying?

                    KENT
          Not really... It's kind of nice to
          have something that makes our town
          unique. Something special to call
          our own... DC comics even made it
          official on January 21, 1972.
          Boring you?

                    LO
          Kind of.

                    KENT
          Can I ask your name?

                    LO
          People call me Lo.

(CONTINUED)

                    KENT
          Lo? Short for Lois?

                    LO
          Nope... That would too weird...
          although better than my real
          name... Lola.

                    KENT
          It's a nice name.

                    LO
          If you say so.

                    KENT
          So you're ok then? Need directions
          or anything?

                    LO
          This is where I was going.

                    KENT
          But you're not a fan?

                    LO
          You bug all the tourists like this?

                    KENT
          That's what we do in Metropolis...
          Bug tourists... Have to make sure
          that you're not some villain in
          disguise out to get Superman... (Lo
          looks away annoyed) Still not
          funny... I can take a hint... Have
          a good visit.

(He slowly goes hoping she will stop him)

                    LO
          Sorry... I didn't mean to be a
          pain.

(Kent returns happily)

                    KENT
          You've been traveling... That makes
          people tired. I understand.

                    LO
          I feel like an idiot.

                         KENT
          Why? A lot of people think
          Metropolis should be bigger... In
          fact our founding fathers thought
          our town would be a city one day
          being situated on a major river
          near the junction of four states...

                         LO
          Enough history okay?

                         KENT
          Sorry... got it... Back to you...
          Where were we?

                         LO
          I'm an idiot?

                         KENT
          That's right. I'm listening.

                         LO
          Thanks.

                         KENT
          Anytime... So why you feeling bad?

                         LO
          I came here because of a dream.

                         KENT
          Really?

                         LO
          I had this dream about
          Metropolis... It was more like a
          city but this statue... It's
          exactly the same.

                         KENT
          You ever see pictures?

                         LO
          Never.

                         KENT
          Wild... So why come see it?

                         LO
          Because of something that happened
          in my dream... Something that
          happened at this statue that was
          pretty wonderful. Something I'd
          really like more than anything.

(CONTINUED)

                         KENT
          What?

                         LO
          It will sound dumb.

                         KENT
          Go ahead. You can tell me.

                         LO
          I fell in love.

                         KENT
          Really? Under a Superman statue?

                         LO
          Under this statue.

                         KENT
          You get a good look at the guy?

                         LO
          He had on a Superman shirt.

                         KENT
          Plenty of those around here.. I
          have one... Didn't wear it today
          though... I can go put it on.

                         LO
          Slow down there, Flash... I don't
          think you're the guy.

                         KENT
          Oh...

                         LO
          It can't be the first guy I run in
          to... That's too lucky... Sorry to
          hurt your feelings but I don't feel
          it. The chemistry. The dream had
          a whole lot of chemistry. And an
          explosion.

(She gets lost in thought)

                         KENT
          No worries. Maybe I can help. Tell
          me more about the dream. Maybe I
          know the guy.

                                        (CONTINUED)

                         LO
          Not much more that I remember. Oh
          wait. He had on glasses too.

                         KENT
          Glasses and superman
          shirt. Anything else?

                         LO
          The other thing about the dream
          that was really odd was that I felt
          the urge to cash in my life savings
          too... Something told me I'd need
          it for this trip.

                         KENT
          Your entire life savings. Is
          there... in your purse?

                         LO
          Everything I have is right here.

(They are quiet a minute. Kent is looking at her and she
looks away shyly. Suddenly Kent grabs the purse and runs.
Lo jumps up in shock)

                         LO (CONT.)
          Hey! Wait a minute! Wh...
          what?! No! This isn't right! I
          come to your stupid town and the
          first thing that happens is that
          I'm mugged? First guy I meet and
          he's a con man. Kent the con
          man. Ah! Why am I so
          stupid? Don't talk to
          strangers. Isn't that what you
          teach to kids, Superman? Well, I
          blew it. Blabbed to some random
          dude and he mugs me. Why did I
          follow a dream? I am an idiot. A
          stupid, dumb bubblehead.

(She plops down on a bench)

                         LO (CONT.)
          I'm always a victim. There's not
          enough heroes in this world. Not
          enough Supermans. Sure, there's
          bunches of you parading around in
          costumes, but there's not many real
          men of steel. Not any willing to
          take a bullet for me.

(She jumps up again)

                                        (CONTINUED)

                    LO (CONT.)
        And you know what?! My life
        savings was 50 bucks! How's that
        for irony? And my credit cards are
        maxed out! Ha! Jokes on you!

(Plops down on bench again)

                    LO (CONT.)
        I just want my lucky key chain
        back.

(Simon, a guy in glasses and a button up shirt, enters with
her purse)

                    SIMON
        Is this your purse?

(Lo is so stunned she doesn't know what to say)

                    SIMON (CONT.)
        I didn't mean to go through your
        purse but I needed to find an ID or
        something. I found your driver's
        license. It looks a bit like
        you... but you're... you're
        prettier in person.

                    LO
        Thank you!

(She runs up and hugs him)

                    SIMON
        Tough day?

(She lets go of him and nods)

                    LO
        Very... how did you find it?

                    SIMON
        I tripped the guy who was running
        away with it.

                    LO
        You did?

                    SIMON
        Kind of on accident. I'm a bit of
        a klutz. But I wouldn't give it
        back once I got it. I've known
        Kent for a long time and when you
                    (MORE)

                    SIMON (cont'd)
          see him with a purse, you know he's
          not headed to a superhero
          cross-dressing competition.

(Lo laughs)

                    SIMON (CONT.)
          You have a nice laugh.

                    LO
          I hate my laugh. I snort.

                    SIMON
          It's cute.

                    LO
          So, you from around here?

                    SIMON
          Kind of. I work at the
          SuperMuseum. I wasn't born here
          but I've lived here for a while. I
          stumbled on this little town and
          fell in love with it. I kept
          coming back until I didn't leave
          again.

                    LO
          Something just kind of drew you
          here.

                    SIMON
          Give me Metropolis over Chicago any
          day.

                    LO
          Chicago sucks.

                    SIMON
          And blows.

(They laugh)

                    SIMON (CONT.)
          Want me to show you around?

                    LO
          Sure. I'd like that.

(She takes his arm)

(CONTINUED)

                        SIMON
            We'll do the walking tour. I left
            my cape at home.

                        LO
            You wouldn't happen to have on a
            superman t-shirt would you?

(As they exit)

                        SIMON
            I do actually. Why?

                        LO
            No reason.

(She has a big smile)

                        END OF SCENE

(Alien enters and looks at the statue of Superman)

                        ALIEN
            A mighty hero, from another world.
            He came to protect the people of
            Earth, but he easily could have
            come to conquer. With his power,
            he could have enslaved an entire
            planet, yet he chose to come in
            peace and help the people who cared
            for him as a child. It's a
            wonderful story of first contact,
            with an alien who loved Earth and
            changed the world forever. But not
            all outsiders come in peace. All
            bring change. Earth has been alone
            in the universe too long. At last,
            there will be first contact. The
            moment that would change the lives
            of everyone on an entire planet
            forever. Will it be for the better
            like the tale of Superman? Or will
            be a tale of woe and
            destruction? It may all come down
            to how we greet this first visitor
            from another world. Do we extend
            the hand of kindness, like in the
            tale of this super man? Do we
            comfort the lost child in a time of
            need? Or do we react with fear and
            terror and turn this encounter in
            to something that will alter
            reality forever, leading us down a
            path into the unknown.

PRINCESS FROM ANOTHER PLANET

(In darkness)

                    GENERAL
          Fire!

(Bullets, bombs and explosions are heard. Then silence a
moment)

                    GENERAL (CONT.)
          Retreat!

(Lights come up on an Alien Space Princess)

                    PRINCESS
          Veeble brox not!

                    GENERAL
          Send in the translator.

(A nerdy looking Scientist with a bunch of equipment enters.
A soldier is along side him protecting him as he sets up his
equipment)

                    PRINCESS
          Noow wop not!

(Princess goes toward Scientist)

                    SOLDIER
          You sure that thing is going to
          work?

                    SCIENTIST
          There's one way to find out.

(Scientist turns on machine)

                    PRINCESS
          Your puny weapons have no effect on
          me.

                    SOLDIER
          It worked!

                    SCIENTIST
          Can you understand me?

                    PRINCESS
          I understand your words but not
          your actions. Why did you attack
          me? Why did you insist on
                    (MORE)

(CONTINUED)

                              PRINCESS (cont'd)
                    destroying what you don't
                    understand?

(Scientist turns to solider)

                              SCIENTIST
                    Why were you shooting at her?

                              SOLDIER
                    The general told us to.

                              SCIENTIST
                    "Theirs not to reason why, theirs
                    but to do and die."

                              SOLDIER
                    Huh?

                              SCIENTIST
                    Exactly.

(To Scientist)

                              PRINCESS
                    You seem different. Are you the
                    wise warrior I seek?

                              SOLDIER
                    Warrior?

(He laughs and others can be heard laughing off
stage. Scientist gives them a dirty look)

                              PRINCESS
                    Silence!

(She touches her necklace with one hand and makes a motion
with the other at soldier and he gets pushed back and falls)

                              GENERAL
                    Fire!

                              SCIENTIST
                    No! Wait! I'm right here you
                    idiots!

(Princess touches her necklace with one hand and waves her
other hand)

                              PRINCESS
                    Their weapons are useless now.

                         GENERAL
              Retreat!

(Sound of soldiers, tanks, etc. are heard and then fade
away)

                         SCIENTIST
              You appear to be pretty
              powerful. Why would you need our
              help?

                         PRINCESS
              We may have power but we seek
              wisdom. My quest has brought me
              here. Are you the one?

                         SCIENTIST
              I did graduate at the top of my
              class at Tech.

                         PRINCESS
              Your Earth accolades are
              meaningless to me. What is this
              about your neck?

                         SCIENTIST
              It's just a space rock I found. I
              follow shooting stars and collect
              meteorites.

                         PRINCESS
              Oh follower of shooting stars. May
              I see your stone.

                         SCIENTIST
              Uh... sure.

(He hands it to her)

                         PRINCESS
              This is our message. You found
              it. You must be the chosen one.
              You have the knowledge we need to
              heal our planet.

                         SCIENTIST
              Hey guys! I'm the chosen one!

(Soldier laugh off stage)

                         SCIENTIST (CONT.)
              I really hate those guys.

                                        (CONTINUED)

                    PRINCESS
Do you want me to destroy them?

                    SCIENTIST
Naw... not now. Maybe later.

                    PRINCESS
Why do they mock you?

                    SCIENTIST
I am a nerd... a loser.

                    PRINCESS
But you are an inventor. A creator
of new things. They only destroy.

                    SCIENTIST
That's kind of how it goes
here. We invent and they find a
way to use it to destroy.

                    PRINCESS
We will not treat you so on my
planet. Will you join me? Please
come back to my planet and help us?

                    SCIENTIST
What happened to your planet?

                    PRINCESS
Our air has turned to poison. We
can no longer breath outside and
must hide indoors. The energy that
once gave us light and power now
destroys us.

                    SCIENTIST
Ever try wind or solar power?

                    PRINCESS
Whatever do you mean? How can we
use the wind and sun?

                    SCIENTIST
Wow, this will be easy.

                    PRINCESS
You will be a hero. You will be
rewarded beyond your wildest
dreams.

(CONTINUED)

                        SCIENTIST
          Seeing those soldier scattered was
          a pretty good reward.

                        PRINCESS
          I can vaporize them too if you
          wish.

(She reaches for her necklace)

                        SCIENTIST
          That's very nice of you, but it's
          not necessary. I don't want to
          stoop to their level.

                        PRINCESS
          You are wise. I have chosen
          well. Come with me and save my
          planet.

(Princess takes Scientist's arm affectionately and Scientist
smiles shyly. Nerdy woman, Lila, rushes on stage)

                        LILA
          Wait, Peter. Please don't go!

(Princess turns and stands between Scientist and Lila)

                        PRINCESS
          What is the meaning of this?

                        LILA
          That man there is my Peter... He's
          my boyfriend.

                        PRINCESS
          He is mine now. He has given
          himself to me.

(Lila looks very hurt)

                        LILA
          Peter, is that true?

                        SCIENTIST
          She needs my help. Her planet is
          in trouble.

                        LILA
          How long will you be gone?

                              PRINCESS
                    You may return in a decade or two.

                              LILA
                    What?! 10 years!

                              PRINCESS
                    Or twenty. But I doubt he'll want
                    to return. We'll reward him
                    handsomely and give him anything he
                    wants.

          (Princess goes behind Scientist and touches him
          lovingly. Scientist looks pleased)

                              LILA
                    How could you do this to me, Peter?

                              SCIENTIST
                    Do what?

                              LILA
                    Leave me?

                              SCIENTIST
                    I'll be back. Don't worry.

          (But he's looking at the Princess all dreamy. Lila grabs
          him and pulls him away)

                              LILA
                    Stay away from him. You have him
                    under some kind of spell don't you?

          (Lila puts herself between Scientist and Princess)

                              PRINCESS
                    How dare you! You will face my
                    wrath!

          (Before the Princess can touch her necklace, Lila jumps
          forward and grabs the necklace and yanks it off her neck)

                              PRINCESS (CONT.)
                    What have you done?! You fool?

          (Scientist shakes his head and is startled when he sees
          Princess)

                              SCIENTIST
                    She looks mad.

                         PRINCESS
            Give those back to me!

                         LILA
            I don't think so.

                         PRINCESS
            You are putting yourselves in
            terrible danger. Those jewels
            channel my power. Without them, I
            will lose control.

                         LILA
            I think you lost control long
            ago. How dare you try and take my
            Peter away.

                         PRINCESS
            Please, give them back to me. If
            the power in those are released in
            your world, it will change you
            all...

                         LILA
            I don't care. I won't let you take
            Peter from me. I'll risk
            everything to save him.

                         PRINCESS
            You would risk your entire planet
            for one man.

                         LILA
            Not any man... this man. He's my
            world. I don't need anything else
            but him.

                         SCIENTIST
            Lila... that's the sweetest thing
            you ever said to me.

                         LILA
            Quiet. You're in trouble too
            mister.

                         PRINCESS
            Please... help me, Peter. You're
            my only hope.

                         LILA
            What a drama queen. Let's go,
            Peter.

        (Peter seems torn)

                              LILA (CONT.)
               I know I'm not perfect, but I do
               really love you. She's just going
               to use you. Chew you up, take what
               you have to offer and then spit you
               out. You are just a tool to
               her. A means to an end and then
               she'll cast you aside. You know
               I'm not like that. You know I love
               you for you and not what I can get
               out of you. So... what do you
               chose? A crazy, wild fling that
               will end in ruin or simple, true,
               honest love?

(Lila gives Scientist the jewels and Princess looks hopeful)

                              SCIENTIST
               I chose you, Lila.

(Scientist throws down jewels and stomps on them. Lila is
happy and helps)

                              PRINCESS
               No! What have you done?!

(Lila and Scientist leave and Princess goes to the jewels)

                              PRINCESS (CONT.)
               You have released their power on
               your world. It will change
               everything as you know it. It will
               give some of you powers and make
               others of you go mad. Some of you
               will chose greatness and seek good
               with your new found power, but
               others of you will react with fear
               and anger and go down a path of
               evil.

(Soldier enters cautiously)

                              SOLDIER
               Princess... you are under
               arrest. Please come with me.

                              PRINCESS
               But perhaps there is hope. Perhaps
               there is a Phoenix that will rise
               from these ashes. I will find a
               champion among you whose new found
               powers can be harnessed.

                         SOLDIER
          Yeah, yeah. Save it for someone
          who cares. Let's go, Princess.

                         PRINCESS
          I will have my champion destroy you
          first.

                         SOLDIER
          General! She's being mean to me!

(Exit and lights fade to black)

GROWING UP IS HARD TO DO

(Someone is under a bedroom sheet. He peeks out nervously.
He is in pajamas. The sillier the print on the sheet and
pajamas the better)

                         THAD
          I feel so strange tonight, waking
          up in the full moon's light.
          Something had changed. I am not the
          same. I'm getting really hairy.
          More hairy than I thought a man
          could be. This is rather scary and
          ...and....my voice is changing
          toooooo.

(He howls and then slaps his hands over his mouth)

                         THAD (CONT.)
          Was that a howl? And my hands...
          Look at my nails... did I forget to
          cut them or are they longer... And
          sharper than before?

(He struggles with the sheet.... He gets all wrapped up in a
panic. He claws and rips at it)

                         THAD (CONT.)
          Claws! Actual claws!

(He finally gets free of the sheet)

                         THAD (CONT.)
          Mirror? Where's a mirrorrrrr!

(Big growl)

                                                    (CONTINUED)

                         THAD (CONT.)
               Was that a growl? From my stomach?
               What's there to eat? I could really
               use some meat.

(Holds his stomach)

                         THAD (CONT.)
               Growing up is so hard to do...

(Reaches back And feels something bulging at his rear)

                         THAD (CONT.)
               ....especially when you're growing
               a tail toooooooo!

(He howls and holds his bottom and carefully scoots off
stage)

                         END OF SCENE

A WEREWOLF IN MY BED

Viv sees something under her bed.

                         VIV
               Who's there?

                         THAD
               It's me.

                         VIV
               Thad? What's going on?

                         THAD
               You know how I said I was going
               through some changes?

                         VIV
               Yes.

                         THAD
               Well, it happened.

                         VIV
               What?

                         THAD
               I can't say.

                    VIV
          It's ok... We are all going through
          a lot changes.. We're turning in to
          adults.

                    THAD
          It's a little more complicated than
          that.

                    VIV
          Look.. Whatever you are going
          through... I am here for you... I
          am willing to listen... I will
          never give up on you.

(He comes out... He is a werewolf. She screams and runs
away. He sits in bed sadly and starts nibbling on an itch
on his arm. She eventually comes back in)

                    VIV
          Sorry about that.

                    THAD
          It's ok... I know I am a freak...

                    VIV
          No no no... But what happened?

                    THAD
          I am a werewolf.

                    VIV
          A howl at the moon werewolf? But
          shouldn't you be all crazy slobbery
          and growling? Do you want to bite
          me or something?

                    THAD
          Yes, but not for the reason you
          might think.

                    VIV
          Am I safe?

                    THAD
          Yes... I can control myself... Well
          I can't control the hair... But the
          attitude... I just wanted you to
          know... In case something happened
          to me...

(CONTINUED)

                    VIV
          What? What might happen?

                    THAD
          Dog catcher... Rancher..... Monster
          hunter. All kinds of dangers.

                    VIV
          There are monster hunters?

                    THAD
          That's why there are not many
          monsters.

                    VIV
          That's terrible.

                    THAD
          Well... Monsters are called that
          for a reason.

                    VIV
          But not you... You're a vegetarian!

                    THAD
          That's not easy... I get cravings
          every full moon.

                    VIV
          I am so sorry... I promise I won't
          eat meat around you ever again...
          That must be a terrible
          temptation... I shouldn't eat meat
          at all anymore in fact.

                    THAD
          You're so sweet to me.

                    VIV
          You mean so much to me.

(He is struggling)

                    THAD
          I get so itchy.

                    VIV
          Here, I can help.

(She scratches him and he starts thumping his foot)

                                        (CONTINUED)

                    THAD
          Oh yeah. Thank you... That felt
          really good.

                    VIV
          Your fur is kind of soft... I like
          how it smells too.

                    THAD
          Really?

(She smells him again)

                    VIV
          Yeah.

                    THAD
          You're not scared anymore... This
          isn't too weird?

                    VIV
          It is weird and scary but I want to
          see the best in this... I want to
          support you... We can get through
          this together.

                    THAD
          It's something that will always be
          here... I will never get rid of it.

                    VIV
          It's you and that's all that
          matters. And I have secrets too...
          I have baggage too...

                    THAD
          That tops this?

                    VIV
          This isn't a contest. The point is
          that we support each other no
          matter what life throws our way...
          Would you support me if I suddenly
          became a vampire?

                    THAD
          Werewolves and vampires don't get
          along very well.

                    VIV
          So you would just dump me?

                         THAD
            No... Never... I would be here for
            you too... Vampire, zombie,
            mummy... Any kind of creature
            there is inside you... I would
            still be here for you.

(Viv hugs him)

                         VIV
            I knew you would... You wearing
            something? You smell so good.

                         THAD
            Much be a scent I am giving off.
            Probably means I like you.

                         VIV
            You're not going to start marking
            your territory are you?

                         THAD
            Hey!

                         VIV
            Just kidding.

                         THAD
            I would never do that to your
            room... Maybe outside your house...
            But never inside.

                         VIV
            You marked outside my house?

                         THAD
            Can we change the subject?

                         VIV
            Okay...

(They are quiet)

                         VIV
            So.. Why do you mark your
            territory?

                         THAD
            Grrrr.

                         VIV
            Am I your territory?

                    THAD
Maybe... That creep you out?

                    VIV
It's kind of romantic.

                    THAD
Really?

                    VIV
It makes me feel... Important...
Special.

                    THAD
You are special.

                    VIV
Special? In what way?

                    THAD
Special in the best possible way...
I knew you were great but I never
thought you would be okay with
this.

                    VIV
It won't be easy ... Did this start
recently?

                    THAD
No... For a while... That's why I
am never around during a full moon.

                    VIV
But why tell me now? Please tell
me it's because you want to get
more serious.

                    THAD
I wish... I was worried I might
even have to break up.

                    VIV
No! Why?

                    THAD
To keep you safe.

                    VIV
I know you wouldn't hurt me.

(CONTINUED)

                         THAD
          Not from me...

                         VIV
          From other werewolves?

                         THAD
          No, I made sure...

                         VIV
          The marking?   '

(She smiles)

                         THAD
          Can we drop that?

                         VIV
          Fine... So what danger?

                         THAD
          The underground is talking... It
          could just be a rumor.

                         VIV
          Underground?

                         THAD
          It's a system that keeps us hidden
          and safe... That's why you so
          rarely hear about monsters anymore.
          You get renegades like Bigfoot but
          overall it is pretty quiet.

                         VIV
          But something happened?

                         THAD
          There is a rumor of a monster
          hunter... Here in our town.

                         VIV
          Hunter... Like he wants to catch
          you.

                         THAD
          Worse.

                         VIV
          We have to hide you... We have to
          keep you safe. Will we have to
          fight... I can fight.. I am a
          toughie.

                    THAD
          No, I would never put you in
          danger.

                    VIV
          That's up to me isn't it? I am my
          own person... I can chose.

                    THAD
          But you have no clue what you are
          choosing... I don't either... I
          have no clue what we are up
          against.

                    VIV
          I know one thing.

                    THAD
          What's that?

                    VIV
          That I want to be with you... I
          never want to let you go... I never
          want to be without you.

                    THAD
          Then we will face this together.

                    VIV
          Beware all monster hunters... Hurt
          my Wolfie and prepare to feel my
          wraith...

                    THAD
          Very scary.

                    VIV
          Really?

                    THAD
          I got shivers.

                    VIV
          See. Iza toughie.

                    THAD
          You have such big muscles too.

                    VIV
          Iza strong.

(She does a pose)

                                          (CONTINUED)

                    THAD
          And pretty.

                    VIV
          Now now... You stop that.

                    THAD
          No, you are very pretty.

                    VIV
          You're full of baloney.

                    THAD
          The prettiest girl in the whole
          world.

                    VIV
          You're so full of baloney I could
          make a sandwich out of you.

                    THAD
          Cute... You're very cute too.

                    VIV
          Stop it. No. Toughie.

(Viv does her pose)

                    THAD
          You're the best thing that has ever
          happened to me.

                    VIV
          Me too.

(They look at each other... Wanting to kiss but not sure
how. Gun shot is heard... They dive for cover)

                    VIV
          What was that? Firecracker? Car
          backfire?

                    THAD
          I hope so.

                    END OF SCENE

DREAMING OF DRAGONS

                    VIV
     What do you dream about? I dream
     about dragons. All the time. I
     know they're not real but I want
     them to be. Sure, most girls dream
     of unicorns but I... I love
     dragons... And fire.
     I want to ride my dreams in to the
     night sky and fly over the moon.
     Dragons live in dreams. But what
     if we could make our dreams real? I
     could fly away from here and never
     come back. Leave a world of
     worries behind.
     Does that mean the nightmares would
     be real too? Maybe. It's not
     worth it then. My nightmares are
     pretty bad.
     I'll keep the dragons in my dreams.
     I don't need any more nightmares in
     my life.

                 END OF SCENE

CHOCOLATE AND KISSES

Dougie wants to get a chocolate bar he dropped out in
traffic. Dougie wanders around off balance as the sounds of
cars zip by honking. Rescue Woman rushes in saves him and
takes him to sidewalk safely. Dougie enjoys being held by
her.

                    DOUGIE
     You saved me.

                    RESCUE
     You were in quite a jam there.

                    DOUGIE
     Are you...

Rescue Woman does a proud stance.

                    RESCUE
     Rescue Woman!

                    DOUGIE
     Awesome!

(CONTINUED)

                    RESCUE
          I know.

                    DOUGIE
          Wow! You're like prettier in person
          than in your pictures.

Rescue Woman poses for him.

                    DOUGIE (CONT.)
          I mean your pictures are totally
          hot but in person... yow!

                    RESCUE
          I know.

                    DOUGIE
          Can I get a picture with you?

                    RESCUE
          Of course.

Dougie gets out a strange looking camera. He gets next to
her for a selfie. He does a funny pose next to her and takes
a picture with the camera which has a bright flash. Rescue
Woman suddenly looks faint.

                    DOUGIE
          You okay?

                    RESCUE
          I feel strange. Wait... what's
          going on?

She falls to her knees weakly. Dougie giggles and Super
Sheila enters and laughs an evil laugh.

                    SHEILA
          Muwhahahaha!

                    RESCUE
          What is this?

                    SHEILA
          I know your weakness Rescue
          Woman. That camera flash exposed
          you to Gamma radiation.

                    RESCUE
          No!

                         SHEILA
          It cancels out your powers.

                         RESCUE
          Who are you?

                         SHEILA
          I am Super
          Sheila! Muwhahahah! Science over
          supers!

                         RESCUE
          Super Sheila... Isn't that super
          girl? There already is one.
          Shouldn't you be Sheila the Science
          Skank (or Skunk) or something.

                         SHEILA
          Skunk?

                         RESCUE
          Because you stink.

DOUGIE sniffs SHEILA.

                         DOUGIE
          She smells good to me.

                         RESCUE
          You're creepy.

                         DOUGIE
          I know.

                         SHEILA
          I like creepy.

                         DOUGIE
          And I like sexy. And you's super
          sexy Sheila.

                         RESCUE
          That would be a better name too.

                         SHEILA
          I'll consider it.

                         DOUGIE
          Hee hee. Super Sexy.

                         SHEILA
          You're a good minion
          Dougie. Here's your chocolates.

                                          (CONTINUED)

                         DOUGIE
            I like chocolates. But I like
            kisses better.

                         SHEILA
            Not now... not in front of the
            victim.

                         RESCUE
            What do you plan to do with me?

                         SHEILA
            Well... I suppose when the gamma
            radiation wears off you'll get your
            powers back.

                         RESCUE
            Yes.

                         SHEILA
            So we'll have to dispose of you
            quickly.

                         DOUGIE
            Quick, quick, quickly!

                         SHEILA
            Keep an eye on her for me, Dougie,
            while I check my gadget for
            something special for her.

                         DOUGIE
            Special. Oh, I like the sound of
            that.

                         SHEILA
            That's because you're special
            too. Now watch her and you'll get
            another chocolate.

                         DOUGIE
            And a kiss?

                         SHEILA
            Only if you're extra special.

                         DOUGIE
            I'll be extra special. I
            promise. Cross my heart. Hope she
            dies.

Dougie points at Rescue Woman on the last part and
giggles. Sheila does an evil laugh and exits.

                                              (CONTINUED)

                         RESCUE
          Oh, Dougie... you seem like a
          simple soul. Why are you with such
          an evil person?

                         DOUGIE
          I like Sheila. She's... SEXY!

                         RESCUE
          Wouldn't you rather be helping
          people? Doing something good?

Dougie thinks a moment. It looks like it hurts to think.

                         DOUGIE
          Ummm... no. Sheila's fun.

                         RESCUE
          Looks like you get plenty of
          chocolate from her.

                         DOUGIE
          Yes, I do... yummy in my tummy.

                         RESCUE
          I could give you kisses.

                         DOUGIE
          Hmmm... no. Only Sheila kisses for
          Dougie.

                         RESCUE
          Does Sheila give you lots of
          kisses?

                         DOUGIE
          Hmmm.... no. I have to sneak my
          kisses... when she is asleep I
          sneak kisses... and when she is
          watching her favorite shows.

                         RESCUE
          Let me go and I can give you lots
          of kisses.

                         DOUGIE
          No.

                         RESCUE
          Oh... how about something shiny?

                        DOUGIE
          Shiny? And sparkly?

                        RESCUE
          Very sparkly.

                        DOUGIE
          Okay... show me.

                        RESCUE
          Just come closer.

Dougie looks around nervously and moves a little closer.

                        DOUGIE
          Oh... I love sparklies.

                        RESCUE
          Close your eyes and I'll give it to
          you.

Dougie closes his eyes and sticks out his hands. Rescue
Woman sneaks away off stage. Dougie is there alone for a
moment. Sheila enters and sees Rescue is gone. She goes up
to him angrily.

                        SHEILA
          Where is she?!

                        DOUGIE
          Oh... oh... she promised me a
          sparkly.

                        SHEILA
          You idiot!

                        DOUGIE
          Sheila mad. Dougie bad.

                        SHEILA
          Don't cry Dougie. I hate it when
          you cry.

                        DOUGIE
          Dougie bad?!

                        SHEILA
          Would you stop crying for a
          chocolate?

                        DOUGLIE
          Dougie super bad!

                                        (CONTINUED)

                         SHEILA
          Would you stop crying for a kiss?

Dougie stops crying and nods.

                         DOUGIE
          Dougie likes kisses.

                         SHEILA
          Close your eyes.

                         DOUGIE
            Okay.

Dougie closes his eyes and makes kissy lips.

                         SHEILA
          Come closer.

Dougie scoots forward with kissy lips.

She claps the connector of her new machine to his
lips. Dougie opens is eyes, startled.

She turns on the machine and Dougie is shocked. He spazzes
out and then falls to the ground. Sheila leaves. Dougie
finally says:

                         DOUGIE
          Wow! What a kiss!

                    END OF SCENE

SUPERHERO SUPPORT GROUP

Spotlight comes up on a Superhero, Speedo, sitting in a
chair. A figure sits near him but in the darkness.

                         SPEEDO
          I'm fast... so fast no one can see
          me. I thought I had something
          special... something I could help
          people with, but it ended up being
          a joke. Everyone started calling
          me Speedo. That's one of them
          guy's swim suits... not a
          flattering one either... Have you
          seen a guy in a speedo? Yuck.

                         DOCTOR
          How fast are you?

                         SPEEDO
              You know that pen that was in your
              pocket a second ago? Here it is.

                         DOCTOR
              That is fast.

Doctor thinks.

                         DOCTOR (CONT.)
              How about a chocolate fudge candy
              bar... wait... with almonds.

Speedo holds it out to her.

                         SPEEDO
              That's what everyone wants me to
              do... fetch stuff... I should be
              called Errand Boy.

                         DOCTOR
              And that's why you want to get rid
              of your power... this burden that
              haunts you... it ruins your life.

                         SPEEDO
              Yes.

                         DOCTOR
              I can do that for you... I can take
              away this hardship in your life...
              this curse... forever.

Dramatic superhero music Speedo and Doctor exit.

SCENE 1. WAITING ROOM. DAY.

Lights come up on a group of people dressed as superheroes
sitting in a row of chairs in a waiting room.

                         DOGBOY
              Rough.

                         CATCHICK
              Hiss.

                         DOGBOY
              I wasn't barking.

                         CATCHICK
              Oh.

                                                  (CONTINUED)

                         DOGBOY
              I was thinking how rough of a day
              I've had.

                         CATCHICK
              That's why you're here.

                         DOGBOY
              But I have things to do... crime to
              fight. I can't wait around here
              all day.

                         CATCHICK
              You don't have a choice.

                         SMACK
              I can't take it anymore! I have to
              get out of here.

Doctor enters.

                         DOCTOR
              Sit down.

                         SMACK
              You can't stop me. I'm Smack the
              Superstrong! I will smite you!

                         DOGBOY
              Nice tagline!

Smack swings at Doctor but she backs away and then grabs his
ear and twists. Smack falls to the floor in pain.

                         DOCTOR
              There will be no smiting, nor
              biting.

                         DOGBOY
              Grrr!

                         DOCTOR
              Nor scratching.

                         CATCHICK
              Hisss!

                         DOCTOR
              Everyone please wait your turn and
              no more disturbances.

Doctor lets go of Smack. There is a ding and Doctor exits.

(CONTINUED)

                    DOGBOY
          How did she stop you?

                    SMACK
          I don't know.

                    CATCHICK
          Mind powers. She's got mind powers
          more powerful than you can imagine.

Shade comes from behind the chairs.

                    SHADE
          Our powers are useless around her.

                    DOGBOY
          Where'd you come from?

                    SHADE
          I am Shade. I came from the
          shadows.

                    CATCHICK
          More like from behind the
          chairs. How long have you been
          back there?

                    SHADE
          Long enough to know what's going on
          here.

                    DOGBOY
          What is going on?

                    SHADE
          The doctor is removing our powers.

                    SMACK
          What?

                    SHADE
          Not only can she stop us. She can
          take away our powers... (dramatic
          pause) ...forever!

                    DOGBOY
          Nice dramatic pause.

                    SMACK
          This is terrible. I'd be nothing
          without my super strength! I can't
          go back to being some loser working
          at D-Mart.

                                        (CONTINUED)

                         CATCHICK
          Personally I'm tired of all the
          hairballs. She can have my
          powers.

                         DOGBOY
          I do get tired of smelling
          everything.

DOGBOY sniffs around and looks at Shade and makes a face.

                         DOGBOY (CONT.)
          You smell like you've been hiding
          there a LONG time.

                         SHADE
          We have to escape.

                         SMACK
          Or smite the doc!

                         DOGBOY
          But how?

                         SHADE
          Shhh! She's coming!

Shade hides behind the chairs. The others sit in their
chairs. The Doctor enters with another superhero.

                         DOCTOR
          You'll never have to worry about
          flying again.

                         CAPER
          I guess it's time to hang up my
          cape.

                         DOCTOR
          Stay off the rooftops. Or we'll
          have to have another session.

                         CAPER
          I'm done. Please. I promise.

                         DOCTOR
          Very well. No need to schedule a
          followup then.

                         CAPER
          Please. Never again.

                          DOCTOR
          Next!

Catchick stands. Dogboy grabs her arm but she hisses and
pulls away.

                          CATCHICK
          Look. I want to be able to go the
          beach without getting the urge to
          use the bathroom. I want to go
          swimming again. I am tired of all
          those naps. Please doctor. Take
          me next.

                          DOCTOR
          Walk this way.

Catchick follows Doctor off. Caper starts to go but Smack
grabs him. Shade comes out.

                          SMACK
          The doctor took your powers!

                          CAPER
          I think so.

                          SHADE
          Try flying.

                          CAPER
          No, I promised.

                          SHADE
          Get on that chair and try.

                          CAPER
          I don't want to go back in
          there. I promised never to fly
          again. I won't do it. Please don't
          make me. It was horrible.

                          SMACK
          What did the doctor do?

                          CAPER
          I can't say. It... it was too
          terrible.

                          SHADE
          Get on that chair. I must know if
          she really took your powers.

(CONTINUED)

                         CAPER
          No.

                         SHADE
          Do it or else.

                         CAPER
          Or else what?

                         SHADE
          I'll haunt you until the day you
          die. You know I can be pretty
          scary.

                         CAPER
          The doctor is scary. You're just
          super annoying. Fine. Then you'll
          let me go?

                         SHADE
          Of course.

Caper gets on a chair. They watch and Caper jumps and
falls.

                         CAPER
          There. Happy?

                         SHADE
          The Doctor did it. She really can
          take our powers.

Smack grabs Caper.

                         SMACK
          Let's try the window to be sure.

Smack throws Caper through a window. He sticks his head
out. Caper screams. Then there is a thud.

                         SMACK (CONT.)
          Nope. Can't fly.

                         DOGBOY
          Did you have to do that?

                         SMACK
          Yes, yes I did.

                         SHADE
          We had to make sure his powers were
          really gone or if it was the
          temporary power jam of being near
          the doctor.

                                                    (CONTINUED)

Dogboy looks out window.

                    DOGBOY
               But still... did you have to do
               that?

                    SMACK
               He landed on that old lady. He'll
               live.

                    DOGBOY
               What about the old lady?

                    SMACK
               Good point.

Doctor comes out.

                    DOCTOR
               I saw something out my window that
               concerned me.

Shade points at Smack.

                    SHADE
               He did it.

Shade runs and hides behind chairs.

                    DOCTOR
               Are we a little out of control?

                    SMACK
               Yes you are. It's smiting time!

Everyone goes in to slow motion. Smack swings slowly at the
Doctor who dodges slowly. Smack falls past doctor who gives
him a vulcan neck pinch. Everything goes back the regular
motion and Smack passes out. Shade jumps up and points.

                    SHADE
               Alien! The doctor is an
               alien. That was an alien neck
               pinch.

                    DOCTOR
               Do I need to do it to you too?

                    SHADE
               No, no... fading away.

Shade goes behind chairs.

                         DOGBOY
               What is going on here?

                         DOCTOR
               You all have a problem and I have
               the cure.

                         DOGBOY
               Problem?

                         DOCTOR
               Don't you feel a great
               burden? Don't you feel the weight
               of the world on your
               shoulders? You feel like you have
               to deal with all the world's
               evils. But I can change all
               that. No more burdens. No more
               worries.

There is a ding. Doctor leaves.

                         SHADE
               Don't listen to the Doctor. It's
               part of the mind control. You must
               resist.

                         DOGBOY
               I understand what she means
               though. It gets so hard
               sometimes. I feel like there is so
               much evil in the world and there's
               nothing I can do to defeat it.

                         SHADE
               Snap out of it!

Shade slaps Dogboy.

                         DOGBOY
               Grr!

Doctor comes out with Catchick.

                         DOCTOR
               How do you feel?

                         CATCHICK
               Awesome! I'm going surfing! Hang
               ten dudes!

Catchick steps on Smack and exits. Smack wakes up all
dazed. Dogboy helps him in to a chair.

                         DOCTOR
               The weight of the world is off her
               shoulders. She's happy now.

                         SHADE
               Being a hero isn't about
               happiness.

                         DOCTOR
               Then what is it about?

                         SHADE
               It's about changing the world and
               making it a better place.

                         DOCTOR
               And have you changed the world? Is
               it a better place?

                         SHADE
               Well, not yet.

                         DOCTOR
               Anyone can change the world. You
               don't have to have superpowers.

                         SHADE
               I am sooo tired of hearing about
               that Batguy. Give me a few billion
               dollars for gadgets and I'd be
               pretty powerful too.

                         DOCTOR
               I'm saying that ordinary people can
               make a difference in this world.

The heroes look at each other a moment and then laugh.

                         SHADE
               Ordinary people... making a
               difference? HA!

                         DOCTOR
               What about teachers, nurses, police
               officers? They all make a
               difference.

                         SMACK
               Uh...

                         DOGBOY
               She's got a point.

                    SHADE
          Don't listen to her. She's
          twisting your minds.

                    DOCTOR
          Or maybe I'm the hero and I'm the
          one fixing problems.

                    SMACK
          Uh... I hate thinking. My brain
          hurts. Too much talking. Not
          enough smiting.

                    SHADE
          Blah, blah, blah... her words will
          destroy us!

                    DOCTOR
          Or maybe they'll make you better.

                    SHADE
          You'll have to catch me first.

Shade jumps behind chairs again.

                    DOCTOR
          So who's next?

                    DOGBOY
          Will the world really be okay
          without Supers?

                    DOCTOR
          It's time for the world to solve
          their own problems.

                    DOGBOY
          People are so demanding. Always
          wanting more and more. Now they
          just expect me to help. They
          hardly ever say thank you anymore.

                    SMACK
          Lift this, crush that, open that
          jar... I feel so used sometimes.

                    DOGBOY
          A friendly thank you would do or
          even a nice greeting card.

                    SMACK
          Or cookies. I wish someone would
          bake me some cookies. That would
          be all the thanks I need.

                                        (CONTINUED)

Dogboy and Smack start to tear up.

                    DOCTOR
          Supers are the ultimate
          co-dependents. Always looking for
          problems. Never happy if there
          isn't a crisis. Getting themselves
          involved with demanding citizens
          who don't appreciate them for who
          they are. You can never do enough
          to please them.

Dogboy and Smack are crying loudly now.

                    DOGBOY
          It's true. It's never enough.

                    DOCTOR
          Come in, friends. We'll take care
          of all this for you. No more
          stress. No more worries.

Doctor takes Dogboy and Smack in to office. Shade comes out
of hiding.

                    SHADE
          And then there was one. We have
          finally met our match.

Lights fade to black.

SCENE 2

In the waiting room, Catchick now sits no longer in her
costume. She looks like an ordinary citizen. Dogboy
enters, also looking like a regular person.

                    DOGBOY
          Hey there. How are you?

                    CATCHICK
          Fine.

Dogboy is willing to chat but Catchick is not. She looks at
a magazine. Smack enters looking normal as well but very
grumpy. Smack sits next to Dogboy.

                    DOGBOY (CONT.)
          Hey. Do any good smiting lately?

                    SMACK
No... do I know you?

                    DOGBOY
I'm... I was... Dogboy.

                    SMACK
So, how are things for you?

                    DOGBOY
I'm not chasing cars
anymore. That's been nice. How
are you?

                    SMACK
Horrible. Lost my job.

                    DOGBOY
What? Why?

                    SMACK
I was a security guard at a
carnival. But losing my superness
made me lose my edge. I just
couldn't do my job anymore. It's
like I lost something... a piece of
myself that made me better...

                    CATCHICK
Your spirit.

                    SMACK
Yeah!

                    CATCHICK
Our spirit, our mojo... gone.

                    DOGBOY
So... you're not okay?

                    CATCHICK
I'm having a hard time fitting
in. It's hard to be normal.

                    SMACK
Totally. Being crazy was so much
easier.

                    CATCHICK
At least I had an identity. I
don't even know who I am now.

                    SMACK
Totally.

                    CATCHICK
What about you Dogboy?

                    DOGBOY
Doug. My name is Doug.

                    CATCHICK
So how is life... Doug?

                    DOGBOY
It's been better. It's not perfect
but it's been better. I'm not
living in my parent's basement
anymore. I have a job. Not a
great job but I feel good taking
care of myself. I got so wrapped
up in helping others I wasn't
helping myself, but now I am. And
I feel better and people are
treating me better too.

                    CATCHICK
Must be nice.

                    DOGBOY
But I thought you were happy going
to the beach, surfing... no more
hairballs?

                    CATCHICK
But I can't swim. Nearly
drowned. And when I did learn to
swim... there was this
shark. Catchick would have had
that shark for lunch but as Sissy
Jones, I was nearly eaten.

                    SMACK
Sissy?

                    CATCHICK
Yes, my real name is Sissy. I hate
it.

                    SMACK
My real name is Marvin. The name
Marvin strikes fear in no one.

                                        (CONTINUED)

                         DOGBOY
          So you both miss being Supers?

                         SMACK
          I miss being special.

Shade appears from behind the chairs.

                         SHADE
          Then be super again.

Dogboy and Smack jump up in surprise.

                         DOGBOY
          You're still hiding?

                         SHADE
          I'm trying to bring down the doctor
          and her evil plan to rid the world
          of Supers.

                         CATCHICK
          But we're not Supers. We're all a
          bunch of nut jobs.

                         SHADE
          That's what she wants you to think.

Doctor enters. Shade hides.

                         DOCTOR
          Thank you all for coming to the
          support group today. We'll meet
          out here today. Have a seat
          everyone. I want to all talk
          together so we can help each other.

Doctor and others put chairs in a half circle. Shade's
hiding spot is revealed.

                         DOCTOR (CONT.)
          Please join us, Jack.

                         SMACK
          Jack? Dang... cool name.

                         SHADE
          I am the Shade!

                         DOCTOR
          Jack here hasn't been through the
          same therapy as the rest of
          you. You have to be willing to
                         (MORE)

                                          (CONTINUED)

                    DOCTOR (cont'd)
          change for the therapy to work, but
          I was hoping if he saw how well the
          rest of you were doing, then he'd
          be convinced this is for the best.

                    SHADE
          You'll never defeat me,
          Doctor. Never!

                    DOCTOR
          Then you won't mind sitting and
          listening if you have nothing to
          fear.

                    SHADE
          Fear? I'm not afraid.

                    DOCTOR
          Prove it. Sit.

Shade reluctantly joins the others in the half circle and
sits.

                    DOCTOR (CONT.)
          I appreciate you all coming
          today. I've formed this support
          group to help you through this
          transition period to a normal life.

                    CATCHICK
          What is this? Crazy Anonymous?

                    SHADE
          Super Anonymous. Amazing
          Anonymous. League of Extraordinary
          Anonymity.

                    SMACK
          Cool.

                    DOCTOR
          Not cool. No leagues. Nothing
          amazing... just regular people
          sitting down together.

                    CATCHICK
          Amazing was so much better.

                    SMACK
          I lost my job, Doc. How is that
          good?

                    DOCTOR
          It takes time.

                    SMACK
          Time? Much longer and I'll be
          living in a box.

                    SHADE
          See Doctor. Your evil plan only
          brings doom upon us.

                    DOCTOR
          You don't feel doomed, do you Doug?

                    DOGBOY
          No... things are a little better.

                    SHADE
          But not special.

                    CATCHICK
          Exactly... people might have
          thought I was crazy but they
          respected me.

                    SMACK
          R-E-C-T-P... that's what it means
          to me... you said it, sister.

                    DOCTOR
          Sissy.

                    SMACK
          Whatever.

                    CATCHICK
          And I felt like I had a
          purpose. Now I feel empty.

                    DOCTOR
          That's why we're here. To fill you
          with something new.

                    SHADE
          More experiments! I knew it!
          She'll replace our blood with alien
          goo!

                    DOCTOR
          I have developed a twelve step
          program for all of you.

(CONTINUED)

                    CATCHICK
          You're kidding, right?

                    DOCTOR
          Step one... we admit we do not have
          super powers and that believe in
          super powers had made our lives
          unmanageable.

                    SMACK
          Too many words.

                    CATCHICK
          But some of our lives are not
          better.

                    DOCTOR
          They will be soon.

Caper bursts in to the room.

                    CAPER
          Where is the doctor?!

                    CATCHICK
          Another satisfied customer.

                    DOCTOR
          What seems to be the matter? Are
          you here to join our group?

                    CAPER
          You ruined my life.

                    CATCHICK
          That is the theme of the day.

                    DOCTOR
          Now Carl. Calm down and join the
          circle.

                    CAPER
          Your circle of evil!

                    SHADE
          Well said.

                    CAPER
          Shut up! All of you. Just shut...
          up!

                    SMACK
          Good rage. Nice.

                    CAPER
          You all prattle on like villains.

                    CATCHICK
          Hey now!

                    CAPER
          Zip it!

                    CATCHICK
          Or else what fly boy?

                    CAPER
          Or this!

He throws open his cape and reveals a bomb. Everyone jumps
up and backs away.

                    DOCTOR
          Carl, please. Let's talk about
          this.

                    CAPER
          Talk, talk, talk. That's all you
          do... talk, talk, talk... so much
          my head hurts! Now it's my turn.
          Tick, talk, tick, talk.

                    SHADE
          Nice play on words.

                    CAPER
          Thanks. I should have listened to
          you Shade. You were right about
          the doctor here. She's pure evil.

                    SHADE
          Let's take her in.

                    CAPER
          No, I'm going to be rid of her
          forever. Rid of all of
          you. Throwing me out a
          window. How could you?!

                    SHADE
          You don't need to kill
          anyone. We'll let justice take
          it's course.

                                              (CONTINUED)

                         CAPER
               They need proof, Shade. They need
               evidence. She'll just sweet talk
               her way out of it.

                         DOCTOR
               Carl, I'm a doctor... nothing else.

CAPER holds up trigger for bomb.

                         CAPER
               Tick, talk! Tick, talk!

                         CATCHICK
               Doc... I think that's your cue to
               shut up!

                         CAPER
               You can go, Shade. I have no
               quarrel with you.

Shade pauses and looks at others. They look at him
pleadingly.

                         SHADE
               Okay.

Shade runs out.

                         CATCHICK
               Some hero he turned out to be.

                         CAPER
               Now, Doc. Give us back our powers.

                         DOCTOR
               I can't.

                         CAPER
               Liar!

                         SMACK
               Don't make him angry, Doc.

During all this, Dogboy is making his way around behind
Caper unnoticed.

                         CAPER
               I'm way past angry. I'm beyond
               rage.

                          SMACK
                He got my power!

                          CAPER
                I'm ready blow you all sky high...
                it's your play, Doctor.

                          CATCHICK
                Do something, Doc!

                          DOCTOR
                Let the rest of them go, Carl...

                          CAPER
                Caper! Call me Caper.

                          DOCTOR
                I refuse to call you by a name that
                isn't you.

                          CATCHICK
                Come on, Doc! Humor the guy.

                          DOCTOR
                I refuse to back down on my
                principles even in the face of
                death...

                          CATCHICK
                Great.

                          CAPER
                The Doctor is trying score points
                for the afterlife which she'll soon
                be seeing.

Caper holds up the trigger with a shaking hand. Catchick
sees Dogboy circling and helps distract Caper.

                          CATCHICK
                Wait! Can I have one last request?

                          CAPER
                What?

                          CATCHICK
                I'm young... I haven't lived my
                life.

                          CAPER
                What are you talking about?

                         CATCHICK
          There's so much life I want to
          live. So much I want to do... did
          I really do you such a wrong that I
          can't have one little request
          before I die.

                         CAPER
          I don't know...

                         CATCHICK
          Please...

                         CAPER
          What is it?

                         CATCHICK
          It's embarrassing... can I whisper
          it in your ear?

                         CAPER
          Um... I guess so...

Catchick leans in to whisper in his ear and gets hold of his
arm. Dogboy makes his move. Sirens are heard.

                         CAPER (CONT.)
          Sirens! Shade!

                         CATCHICK
          Now!

Catchick wrestles Caper's arm and Dogboy tackles Caper to
the ground. The Doctor cowers between some chairs.

                         DOGBOY
          Got him!

Smash is at the window.

                         SMASH
          Shade brought the cops.

Dogboy struggles to get bomb off.

                         DOGBOY
          Come hold this guy down for us,
          Smash.

                         SMASH
          I'll do you one better.

Smash comes over and rips bomb off Caper, picks him up,
carries him to window.

                                                    (CONTINUED)

                              CAPER
                    No! Wait!

                              SMASH
                    Tic toc, times up!

Smash tosses him out the window. Catchick runs to window.

                              CATCHICK
                    Catch coppers!

Dogboy, Catchick and Smash laugh and cheer.

                              DOGBOY
                    We should form a team!

                              CATCHICK
                    The Superhero Support Group.

                              SMASH
                    I like it.

They notice the Doctor cowering trying to make chairs in to
a little fort.

                              DOGBOY
                    She doesn't look so good.

                              CATCHICK
                    She needs a doctor.

They laugh and exit to dramatic superhero music. As lights
fade.

                              DOCTOR
                    I'll get you next time.

Doctor starts with a weak crazy laugh that gets stronger and
stronger as the lights go to black until it amplifies and
echoes.

                              THE END

SUPER DEAD MAN

In darkness, a huge blast is heard and a cry of pain and
then a huge crash like something hit the ground. Lights
come up on a small crater with a superhero lying in the
middle of it. People rush out to see. A shocked lady is
standing with half a leash next to the crater.

                                              (CONTINUED)

                              GEM
                    What in the holy high heck happened
                    here?

                              HANK
                    Is that?

                              GEM
                    It is!

                              HANK
                    That super hero guy? The one we
                    keep hearing about in the news?

                              WINNY
                    My... my...

She burst out crying.

                              GEM
                    Did he land on your dog?

                              WINNY
                    Uh-huh.

                              GEM
                    You poor thing.

                              WINNY
                    My... my Boopsie!

Gem hugs Winny.

                              HANK
                    He must have fallen down from
                    pretty high to make this size
                    crater.

                              GEM
                    I hear he's strong. Maybe it's
                    just cause he's strong that he made
                    such a big hole.

                              WINNY
                    And crushed my Boopsie!

                              HANK
                    I wonder what he was doing up
                    there?

Sidekick runs in.

                                              (CONTINUED)

                         SIDEKICK
          No!!!!!

Sidekick dramatically falls at superhero's side.

                         GEM
          Hey, you know what happened?

                         WINNY
          Why did he fall on my doggy? That
          was a registered Chow Chow. She
          won prizes. But not any more.

Winny cries.

                         SIDEKICK
          Have some respect lady? This was
          the Earth's greatest hero! Do you
          know how many times he saved this
          planet?

                         HANK
          Nope... no clue.

                         GEM
          Can't recall.

                         SIDEKICK
          You're kidding right? You don't
          know about the aliens?

                         HANK
          Aliens? Really?

                         SIDEKICK
          Or the asteroid?

                         GEM
          Must have missed that on the news.

                         HANK
          You watch the news?

                         GEM
          Entertainment Tonight... The Daily
          Show... Late Late Show... those
          count.

                         SIDEKICK
          No!

                                              (CONTINUED)

                    HANK
I love the Late Late Show.

                    GEM
That skeleton is hilarious.

HANK and GEM laugh, hold out their right arms and shake
their right hands limply.

                    SIDEKICK
What is wrong with you people?!

                    WINNY
Can't you see we're upset? Have
you no respect? It's not easy
losing a pet, is it?

                    SIDEKICK
This wasn't a pet! He was the best
thing that ever happened to this
planet... and now... he's...

                    HANK
Toast.

                    GEM
A hero pancake.

                    HANK
Hero speed bump.

                    SIDEKICK
Stop it!

                    GEM
Touchy touchy.

                    WINNY
So you're affiliated with this
person?

                    SIDEKICK
Yes.

                    WINNY
Then you will be hearing from my
lawyer!

                    SIDEKICK
What?!

                                        (CONTINUED)

                         WINNY
          Your associate killed my prize dog
          and now I demand justice.

                         SIDEKICK
          Why do we even bother? You people
          make me sick. The one person who
          kept you safe from all the dangers
          in the universe and all you can
          worry about is your stupid
          dog! And make jokes! Why did he
          even bother saving you people. You
          all deserve to die!

They all look at Sidekick in shock. They are all quiet for
a bit. A police officer enters in a hurry.

                         WINNY
          Thank goodness, officer. You must
          arrest this person!

Officer points gun at Sidekick.

                         OFFICER
          This the killer?

                         SIDEKICK
          No! I'm his sidekick.

                         OFFICER
          Sidekick? What's that mean? That
          slang for something.

GEM and HANK snicker. Officer smiles like he made a good
joke.

                         SIDEKICK
          Come on! This is serious!

                         WINNY
          I would say so. Officer... this
          person killed my dog.

                         OFFICER
          What? Is this true?

                         SIDEKICK
          Isn't anyone worried about a mighty
          hero is dead here?

                         OFFICER
          Not if he killed some dog, I'm
          not. That's animal cruelty.

                         HANK
          And hunting without a license.

                         GEM
          Dog-a-cide!

                         SIDEKICK
          No! No! No! He's the good guy. He
          saves people.

                         OFFICER
          There's no excuse for animal
          abuse.

                         SIDEKICK
          I... what?! No!

                         OFFICER
          You part of this?

                         SIDEKICK
          Me?

                         WINNY
          That's his partner.

                         OFFICER
          Partner in crime?

                         SIDEKICK
          I can't believe this is
          happening. You're all a bunch of
          stupid, idiotic imbeciles!

                         OFFICER
          Who you calling stupid?

                         SIDEKICK
          That's it! I'm done being a
          hero! I quit!

Sidekick rips off mask, throws it down on super person in
crater and stomps away.

                         WINNY
          Aren't you going to arrest anyone?

                         OFFICER
          I don't think I can cuff that one
          in the crater. Not sure I see an
          arm left.

                                              (CONTINUED)

                         WINNY
          What about the other one?

                         OFFICER
          I suppose I could.

                         WINNY
          Quit supposing and do it!

                         OFFICER
          Geez lady. Fine. I'm going.

Officer exits after Sidekick.

Evil laugh is heard. Mezmero enters in a cool looking
villain uniform with a helmet covering his face. Darth Vader
type breathing comes from his helmet. Hank and Gem are
impressed.

                         HANK
          Now that's impressive.

                         GEM
          Totally.

                         MEZMERO
          I know.

He flips open or removes his helmet and does an evil laugh
again. Hank and Gem are so impressed they clap.

                         MEZMERO
          Please... Control yourselves.

                         GEM
          Sorry... You're just so...

                         MEZMERO
          Handsome? Awesome? Amazing?

                         HANK
          Cool!

                         MEZMERO
          Of course.

Sidekick runs in a yells.

                         SIDEKICK
          No! Not Mezmero! I should have
          known you were behind this!

                                                      (CONTINUED)

                         GEM
          Isn't he impressive?

                         SIDEKICK
          He's pure evil!

                         MEZMERO
          You say the sweetest things.

                         SIDEKICK
          But good should win in the end.
          Evil can't win. That's impossible.

                         MEZMERO
          Get used to it, kid. Can't you hear
          the winds of change?

Mezmero does a heroic stance and farts. Gem and Hank
laugh. Sidekick waves hand at the smell.

                         SIDEKICK
             Evil!

Mezmero does an evil laugh.

Officer enters and Sidekick screams and runs away.
Officer chases Sidekick.

GEM and hank go up to Mezmero.

                         GEM
          Can we get a picture with you?

                         MEZMERO
             Certainly.

They do silly poses with him.

                         HANK
          Thanks! These will be awesome on
          tweetface.

                         MEZMERO
          Be sure to tag them with
          #mezmeroisevil that will link it to
          my fan club

                         GEM
          Sure!

                         HANK
          Bad guys are so cool.

Gem and hank exit. Mezmero stands over super dead man.

(CONTINUED)

                         MEZMERO
          I finally did it. I finally beat
          you. And all I had to do is NOT
          reveal my evil plan. Why do we
          villains always do that? Why do we
          have this strange need to tell you
          all our devious plots before we do
          them? That always gives you time
          for that last minute save... That
          last minute effort that gets you
          through... Or perhaps we reveal
          some flaw in our plan you are able
          to exploit. Not this time. This
          time it was kill first, gloat
          later. This is so much better. I
          get to brag now. Bragging is so
          much better than revealing the
          plan. Time for a victory dance on
          your grave!

Mezmero does a dance around super dead mans hole in the
ground. A kid, DAVID, enters.

                         DAVID
          Stop that!

Mezmero stops.

                         MEZMERO
          What's wrong kid?

                         DAVID
          Show some respect, creep.

                         MEZMERO
          Beat it kid. I am having a moment.
          You're harshing my buzz.

                         DAVID
          You are a bad bad person.

                         MEZMERO
          Yes.

                         DAVID
          And you killed a very great man.

                         MEZMERO
          Great? A great pain in the
          asteroid.

DAVID
He was trying to help the world.
You were trying to destroy it.

MEZMERO
Too late kid. No one cares. All
they see is how amazing I am. It's
all about appearances. No one
remembers an old hero the minute
something new cool and interesting
comes along. He's yesterday's
news... And tomorrow's garbage.

Mezmero laughs at his own joke.

DAVID
Stop that!

DAVID sprays something at Mezmero. Mezmero coughs.

MEZMERO
What was that?

DAVID
Pepper spray.

MEZMERO
No!

Mezmero coughs... Has asthma.

MEZMERO
Where's my inhaler?

DAVID
Not so tough now huh?

MEZMERO
You... You...

DAVID
Yes?

MEZMERO
You're... Evil...

Mezmero dies and falls in to hole with super dead man.

DAVID
Never take off your helmet dude.
Your only weakness. Everyone knows
that. You all have a weakness don't
you. Some fatal flaw. Super dead
(MORE)

                              DAVID (cont'd)
                    man's was a rare Amazon frog poison
                    that every bad guy always seems to
                    dig up. Yours was breathing... Yet
                    you always take off your helmet...
                    Talking is every bad man's
                    weakness. The more super you are,
                    the harder you fall.

Picks up Mezmero's helmet.

                              DAVID (CONT.)
                    Evil huh? Mezmero called me evil.
                    Perhaps we are all a little evil...
                    Battling the good inside us...which
                    side of me won... Did I do the
                    greater good? Does the end justify
                    the means? Or was what I did just
                    as evil?

Sidekick runs in.

                              SIDEKICK
                    You did it! You stopped
                    Mezmero! Way to go kid!

                              DAVID
                    Beat it loser.

David puts on helmet and leaves.

                              SIDEKICK
                    Geez. Who are
                    you? Emo-boy? What's your
                    power? Are you sadder than a
                    speeding bullet? Able to depress
                    people in a single bound? You're
                    like opposite that evil clown
                    villain. Hey, you could defeat
                    him. That's a great idea. You
                    should do battle. Hey! Don't you
                    need a sidekick?

Sidekick follows David off. Officer enters out of
breath. Tries to call out after Sidekick but bends over
unable to speak. Officer sits by the hole. Finally can
talk again after a bit.

                              OFFICER
                    What a mess. That's the problem
                    with you supers. Always leaving a
                    super mess for us to clean
                    up. Things were so much simpler
                              (MORE)

                              OFFICER (cont'd)
          before all you supers
          arrived. Seems like when you're
          all fighting, things get a whole
          lot worse. Would those villains
          really be messing so much up if
          they didn't have one of you super
          guys to beat? Do you supers have
          to break so much to get the bad
          guy. Good vs. evil used be about
          detecting stuff and solving the
          mystery. Now it's about blowing
          things up and who can leave the
          biggest hole in the ground. Give me
          a few good police officers any day
          of the week.

                         END OF SCRIPT

CLOSING MONOLOGUE

                              ALIEN
          In the end, what kind of heroes do
          we desire? Ones who become better
          than us or ones we can
          become? There are heroes all
          around us, doing things every day
          to make our lives a little better.
          These heroes are normal people with
          no super powers but are super in
          other ways. So what path will you
          chose? Will you be an ordinary
          hero who makes a small difference
          in the lives of those around
          you? Or will you settle for
          nothing less than
          extraordinary. But would you chose
          to be super good if it meant you
          would unleash something super bad
          upon the world?

                         END OF PLAY

CAST OF CHARACTERS

SCENE 1: MONOLOGUE FROM ANOTHER WORLD

ALIEN - Narrator throughout the play

SCENE 2: TOUCHED BY AN ALIEN

                                              (CONTINUED)

CAPTAIN and COMMANDER - space explorers who set out to conquer to universe while enjoying a good cup of tea

CADET - young space explorer who has something to prove

GRUNT - old space explorer who prefers a good fight

ALIEN - native of the planet they visit who is captured

SCENE 3: PROTECTO

PROTECTO - Kid who wants to be a hero

SCENE 4: STUNG

JUNE - woman who wants to enjoy nature but nature doesn't like her

PROTECTO - a kid who wants to help

MOLLY - a woman who has no clue how to help

DON - a cranky old man

SCENE 5: BLINDED BY THE KNIGHT

JOE - comic book store owner

ASHLEY - teen beauty queen

HOWARD - a nerdy guy who likes comics and Ashley

NINJA - a teen girl who doesn't like Ashley

DOC - a doctor (can be played by Alien)

SCENE 6: MAN OF METROPOLIS

KENT - A local man from Metropolis

LO - A woman in search of true love

SIMON - a nice guy who befriends Lo

SCENE 7: PRINCESS FROM ANOTHER PLANET

GENERAL - a battle hungry general who would rather shoot first and ask questions later

PRINCESS - a princess from another planet who seeks help from Earth

SOLDIER - a guy who is just following orders

(CONTINUED)

SCIENTIST - a man with the key to helping the princess's planet

LILA - the girlfriend of the scientist who doesn't want the princess to take him away

SCENE 8: A WEREWOLF IN MY BED

THAD - a teen who has turned to a wolf

VIV - the girlfriend of Thad who wants to protect him

SCENE 9: CHOCOLATE AND KISSES

DOUGIE - a dim-witted evil henchman

RESCUE - a local superhero

SHEILA - an evil villain who wants to stop Rescue woman

SCENE 10: SUPERHERO SUPPORT GROUP

SPEEDO - a super fast superhero with problems

DOCTOR - a doctor with the ability to take away super powers

DOGBOY - a dog-like superhero

CATCHICK - a cat-like superhero

SMACK - a super strong superhero

SHADE - a superhero who can hide in the shadows

CAPER - a flying superhero

SCENE 11: SUPER DEAD MAN (7 of any gender)

GEM - ordinary citizen

HANK - ordinary citizen

WINNY - old person who has her prize dog crushed by super dead man

SIDEKICK - stressed out sidekick of super dead man

OFFICER - police officer who finds supers annoying

MEZMERO - cool looking bad guy in a helmet

DAVID - smart kid who defeats Mezmero

Made in the USA
San Bernardino, CA
10 January 2020